CW00687612

Also by Noel Monahan

POETRY

Opposite Walls (Salmon, 1991)

Snowfire (Salmon, 1995)

Curse of the Birds (Salmon, 2000)

The Funeral Game (Salmon, 2004)

PLAYS

Half A Vegetable, a dramatic presentation of Patrick Kavanagh's poetry. Performed by Temenos Theatre, 1994.

Feathers of Time. Performed at Ramor Theatre by St. Clare's College.

Broken Cups. Directed by Aidan Mathews, for RTE Radio 1 Drama, 2002.

Talking Within. Directed by Padraig McIntyre at Ramor Theatre, 2003.

Where Borders Begin. Commissioned by Cavan County Council, 2004.

To Walk On The Wind. Performed at Ramor Theatre by St. Clare's College.

The Children of Lir. Directed by Padraig McIntyre for Livin Dred Theatre, 2007.

BOOKS EDITED & CO-EDITED

Cathal Buí Selected Poems & Short Stories. Co-edited by Noel Monahan & Jim Nolan, 2001.

Badal, Knocknarea Writers Anthology. Edited by Noel Monahan, 2003.

Windows Publications, Authors & Artists Series, Nos. 1-9. Co-edited by Heather Brett and Noel Monahan.

Garden of Golden Apples. Edited by Noel Monahan for the students of St. Daigh's School, Inniskeen, Co. Monaghan, 2009.

Curve of the Moon

Curve of the Moon
NOEL MONAHAN

salmonpoetry

Published in 2010 by
Salmon Poetry
Cliffs of Moher, County Clare, Ireland
Website: www.salmonpoetry.com
Email: info@salmonpoetry.com

ISBN 978-1-907056-38-3

Cover artwork: *The Moon And The Owl (oil on canvas)* by *Pádraig Lynch*
Cover design & typesetting: *Siobhán Hutson*
Printed in England by imprint*digital*.net

Salmon Poetry receives financial assistance from the Arts Council

For my family

Acknowledgements

Acknowledgement is due to the following, in which a number of these poems first appeared:

"Amen Woman" – published in *Something Beginning With P*, edited by Seamus Cashman (The O'Brien Press).
"Marrakech", published in *Poetry Ireland Review*, edited by Paul Muldoon.
"Gathering Mushrooms" and "Scarecrow Woman", published in *Ambit*, London.
"Beyond The Wind" – published in *From Inniskeen To Parnassus* (Patrick Kavanagh Centre & Carrickmacross Arts).
"Boochalawn Buí" – Prize Winning Poem in the Hiberno-English Poetry Award UCD. Published in *Salmon: A Journey In Poetry* (Salmon Poetry, 2007).
"The Separator" – short-listed in the Hiberno-English Poetry Award, UCD.
"A Ghostly Letter From Sheridan To Swift" – shortlisted in The Kilkenny Swift Competition, and published in *The Spark*.
"Reply From The Last Duchess" – published in *Clifden Anthology*.
"Drama Festival" – published in *Cavan Drama Festival Programme*.
"Buskins In The County Museum" – published in *Giving Voice*, No. 1, Caomhnú Broadsheet.
"The Calf-Bearer" – published in *Poetry New Zealand* No. 38.
"Postojina Cave, Slovenia" – published in *The Stony Thursday Book*, Limerick, editor Thomas McCarthy.
"Confession Box" – published in, *Revival 4*, Limerick.
"Black Loaves" – published in *The sHOP* and in *The Best of Poetry 2009*. Edited by Paul Perry.
"The Music of Snow" – read on RTE Radio 1 Christmas Special, presented by Pat Boran.
"Talking To My Shadow" – published in *Orbis* (England).
"Maithiúnas Na bPeacaí" – published in *An Guth 3* (Coiscéim).
"Bealtaine" – published in *An Guth 4* (Coiscéim).
"Ciaróg Dhubh" – published in *An Guth5* (Coiscéim).
"Diary Of A Town" – an extract entitled Mickey Maguire, won The Irish Writers Union Prize for Poetry. A number of extracts were read on Sunday Miscellany, RTÉ Radio 1 and Shannonside/Northern Sound. Also a number of extracts were published in *The Clifden Anthology*, *The Anglo Celt*, *The Longford Leader* and *Virtual Writer* (www.virtualwriter.net). Livin Dred Theatre Company performed a professional dramatization of a number of extracts, directed by Padraig McIntyre.

Thanks to Jessie Lendennie, Salmon Poetry, Joseph Woods, Poetry Ireland, Niall MacMonagle, Seamus Hosey, RTÉ, Heather Brett, Catriona O'Reilly, Martin Donohoe and Cavan County Council for their encouragement.

A special thanks to artist Pádraig Lynch for his painting which appears on the cover of this collection.

Contents

1   Black Loaves

Black Loaves   13
A Ghostly Letter From Sheridan To Swift   14
Reply From The Last Duchess   16
Amen Woman   17
Haiku Devotions   18
Confession Box   19
Paper Chase   20
The School Pond   22
The Back Garden   23
Sleeping Out   25
Catalogue Of My Room   26
Bellavally Gap   27
Feast Of Asses   28
Crom   29
Catching Each Other By The Tail   30
Marrakech   32
For Billy, Kathleen and Family   34
Olive Blossom   35
November Moon   36
December Evening   37
Curve Of The Moon   38
The Music Of Snow   39

2   Beyond The Wind

Beyond The Wind   43
Boochalawn Buí   44
Visiting Kierkegaard's Grave   45
Drama Festival   46
Buskins In The County Museum   47
Gathering Mushrooms   48
The Separator   49
To See September Through A First Year's Eyes   50

The Child Lives Forever Deep Within Us   51
Epithalamium   52
Postojina Cave, Slovenia   53
The Calf-Bearer   54
Talking To My Shadow   55
Cuilcagh   56
Etna   57
Sheela Na Gig   58
Scarecrow Woman   59
Summer Holiday   60
Primal Loss   61
Evening Prayer   62

3   Dánta i nGaeilge agus Aistriúcháin /
Poems in Irish and Translations

Bealtaine   64
The Month Of May   65
Maithiúnas na bPeacaí   66
Forgiveness Of Sins   67
Ciaróg Dhubh   68
Cockroach   69

4   Diary Of A Town   73
(A dramatic poem)

About the author   *119*

1
Black Loaves

Black Loaves

We weren't given the game.
Somewhere, out there in the dark dust
Of childhood, we found it, discovered it bit by bit
And it led us on to making bread,
Baking black loaves, whenever the sun shone.

It was a summer of black clouds
But we were somewhere else,
Where nothing mattered much,
Below in the turf shed by the road,
Mould and water devouring us,
Sifting the turf mould into flour,
Mixing the black dough, sand buckets full of water,
Our postures changing, kneeling upright,
Sitting on hunkers …

Cheerful chatter, half listening to one another.
Dorry said she loved me and might marry me
Some other summer. Swallows flew in and out.
The dog stretched before us, her paws forward,
Eyes wide open, tail wagging,
Watching us mix the mould,
The black dough slipping through our hands.
Des lost concentration for a while
And drew a face in the turf mould with his finger.
Jimmy, who was working in the yard, shouted in at us:
What are you doing, bedaubing in there?

Our hearts were full of black brilliance then.
Trays of turf loaves baking in the sun
Soon crumbled back to mould
But I still feast on the crumbs.

A Ghostly Letter From Sheridan To Swift

Dear Hypothetical Reader, Mon Frère,

Let me Swiftly take you away
To ghostly noise of yesterday,
And you must bend your eyes and ears
To songs and rhymes of bygone years.
     Buffoonery and jugglery,
     Idiosyncratic – octosyllabic.
A poem's meaning, sense and sound
The likes of which can still be found.

Quilca House, Two Thousand and Four
Shades of Sheridan's and Swift's lore,
Ghosts hover here, words all alone,
Silence the language of the stone.
Years have passed since last we conversed,
Before they walked behind our hearse,
Jonathan … Come Back To Quilca,
For one long last noisy fracas …
We'll visit Shantemon, invoke
And get the old altar to smoke,
By Quilca's lake and Stella's bowers,
We'll pluck amaranthine flowers,
Big Doughty will carry your pony,
Brobdignag farmer from Raffony.
You remember how the Teagues could gabble,
Triall, Droch and *Drib* from the Gaelic rabble.

'Tis all changed – all different now
' Twould put the cat off her *Meow*.
Bobby Yahoo has won the elections,
Political and other connections.
It is his vile most burning ambition
Build Piggeries without Planning Permission.

Men happy with the change of life.
Every woman, anyman's wife,
Sex in abundance, they say it's better,
Everyone praises The French Letter.
Supermarkets in Virginia Town,
All claim to bring their prices down.
Jane The Monger, Mickey Cooper,
Joe The Dealer, Jim The Weaver
Had visits from The Receiver.
Only Pat The Baker survived the fall
And Dunnes Stores Better Value Beats Them All.

On second thoughts, not much has changed,
It's just a little more deranged.
We still have lunatics and fools
In charge of Faster Learning Schools.
"*The Legion Club*", open to bribe,
Is now "*The Dáil*", curse of the tribe.
Please return to Quilca once more,
In this year Two Thousand and Four,
I hope you will not grieve to see
Sometimes I write as well as thee.
And lastly, it pleases me most to tell,
Though the body be dead, my soul is well.

                    Semper Eadem,
                In this life and the next,
                        Ton Cher Ami,
                        Tom Punsiby.

Reply From The Last Duchess

After Robert Browning's poem

Have you come here to see my bosom heave?
Listen to him prattle on and deceive.
Don't believe a word of what he says. He
Pulls this curtain everyday and talks of me,
Not for your sake. He likes to play the fool
Talks about my wanderings on a mule
About his estate, eyeing the servants.
I was young then, in love with the merchants,
The squires, the butlers, bakers, whoever!
Love to him was a mystery forever.
My portrait takes hold of him, possesses
Him. He gets swallowed up and confesses
His hideous thoughts, envies and desires.
And with the painter Fra Pandolf , conspires
This false impression. *That's my girl*, he'd bray
As though he purchased me some other day,
Oh Yes! he thought I was a work of art,
But I'd have none of it, I was too smart.
Then he got angry, gave a dark command,
Had someone slit my throat and here I am,
Hanging on the wall as if I was alive.

Amen Woman

She was in love with colours,
Streaks in her hair,
Peacock feathers grew in her hat.
November winds danced on her summer dress
And she always said: *Amen, Amen.*

She pushed a wheelbarrow full of gadgets
Through the streets,
Shouting: lamp shades – clothes pegs – sun glasses –
Nibs for pens – bottles for rheumatism;
And finally she would say: *Amen, Amen.*

She could call at any time
Of day or night, front door, back door.
The cat kept a nervous eye on her,
The dog barked furiously
And she calmed him with her *Amen, Amen.*

She told us all the news,
Who was getting married – what happened to Eileen?
And more if you listened –
About Ukulele Joe and his midnight parties
And then she'd say, *Amen, Amen,* and trundle away.

She got lost somewhere
Disappeared in the fog –
Someone said she went to a brother in America,
Others say she was old enough to die,
Grew wings and flew to heaven, *Amen, Amen.*

Haiku Devotions

Antiphone of rain
On the roof, precedes the chant
Of wind in the trees.

The Rain has blue eyes,
Chains of tears locked in grief, slide
Down my window pane.

Necklace of skulls changes
To one of chrysanthemums
A cycle complete.

The open fire drinks
Wine from the setting sun, eats
The bread of the moon.

One pen and three cobs
At one with the white noise of
Feathers in the wind.

Winter petals fall,
Like snow cradles descending
From God's tearful eyes.

Confession Box

That second year at Boarding School
We carried too great a burden
For our souls to bear,
The heaviness of Virgil's *Aeneid*,
Horace's Odes, *Paradise Lost...*
Weighed us down.

We crawled on our hands and knees
Into a confession box,
That lay flat on its back,
Lodged in the debris of waste furniture,
Abandoned in an old shed
That was out of bounds to all.

This tired old confession box
Was our refuge of sinners.
All martyrs to: *Majors*, *Rothmans* and *Carrolls*,
Clank of the wooden shutter pulled across,
We passed cigarettes through the eyes of the grill,
Surrendered to the call of nicotine.

Throughout that second year
We nursed our dwindling self-esteem,
Lying there, where someone once was kneeling,
Wondering what ghosts lay in the cracks
And crevices, the crucifix, still clinging to the boards,
Made us anxious to be on the good side of God.

A small world, we used to say
As we squeezed into our separate boxes.
Adrift, addicted...
And the silence was not silent
And the darkness was luminous
In the confession box in the shed.

Paper Chase

Three athletic boys played hares,
Ran off ahead of us,
Leaving a trail of paper shreds behind.
The rest of us were hounds
And we followed the scent of old newspapers,
Torn copies, old exam sheets .....
Through the fields of:

Lismacanigan,
   Barcony,
      Lisnabrina,
         Aghawonan .....

We ran through fields, barking.
Cows with smoky breath stared at us,
Alarm calls rang out from blackbirds in the hedges,
The wind whined in the gloom of pine trees
About scattered country houses.

We had to cross the Inny.
The river raged, we swallowed
Angry mouthfuls of rusty water.
Our hands and legs blue with the cold,
Our hearts throbbing with fear of pike and eels,
A thousand hands clawing at the far bank,
Shaking ourselves like wet dogs
We left the reeds, went tracking through the rushes.

We entered moods of wishing:
Wishing we were warm and dry,
Wishing we were conjugating Latin verbs,
Wishing the priest in the Wellingtons
Would stop repeating:
That will knock the blubber off you.

Nothing really happened and everything
Happened.
The wind lifted our game to new heights.
A trail of papers darted across the whins,
Gibberish of torn words, lost syllables,
Headed for the sun. No clues left,
Our barking waned to a slow bow-wow-wow,
We sauntered back to the College, over the bridge,
We never caught up with the hares.

The School Pond

Frogspawn appeared mysteriously
In the school pond over night.
All those black specks looking up at us
From the warm wet slimy stuff,
April warming into May
Eggs melting into movement,
Elusive heads and tails darting everywhere.

Here, in this walled-in garden,
Is our chance to connect to something,
Something deeply grounded,
Timeless,
Unfathomable.

We wrestle in classrooms,
Talking to God on the internet,
Longing for something to wish for,
Awash with plans
For panic attacks, mood swings,
Planning and more planning
And for what?
To continue to guess our fate.

While these tadpoles
Grow arms and legs
And leap into a new existence
With that cool frog look of detachment,
An eye for the invisible,
Knowing something we don't.

The frogs are the stoic heroes of our school,
Sitting there by the pond, uncomplaining,
All masters at bridging the gap,
Restoring the magic.

The Back Garden

We shut our eyes to its darkness
When we heard the awful news.
For years after, it was rarely spoken of,
A wilderness of weeds grew about it
Everything was projected onto it.
It became a sort of refuse bin,
A place to hold our past seven years.

Finally, we tackled the dark chaos,
Germinal energy was bursting everywhere.
The sharp music of blades cut the morning,
Slash hooks, strimmers, waged war
Against tribal weeds and roots of briars,
Catapulting cow-parsley, trimming goat's-beard,
Throttling sow-thistle, nipplewort and yarrow.

A field mouse peeped from underneath a stone,
Sentry to a dry pond where goldfish swam,
Infernal mêlée of old rubbish lay in wait
Under several blankets of scutch grass: a hair brush,
A plastic flag, seven Christmas trees,
Two pence in old money, Action Man, a child's do-do …
A robin perched on a sycamore, looking out for worms.

The garden opened its eyes. We looked and listened,
Skeletons of gooseberry and currant bushes
Cracked in our ears as we dragged a canopy of briars
Across their shoulders, old wounds creaked
Like ghosts hiding in the limbs of trees,
Last year's bird's nest, a moon of moss hooped in twigs,
Sang a solitary note.

The back garden, in all its wonder and terror,
Was cooking in the mother pot for seven years,

It appeared to stretch back to an alphabet of clay
Where words lay hidden inside one another.
It took four days and three of us to turn
The pages back and now we are left
Weighing words and raindrops in broad daylight.

Sleeping Out

I spend a summer night on a sun-lounger
Looking up at the moon,
Listening to the whispers of blue shutters,
Hearing the facia boards breathe.
House lights go out, one by one,
Black fields hang down from the hills,
A sudden breeze, melody of leaves,
Flutter of poplars, maples touch one another
In the dark, something is stirring behind the house.
Night voices echo far away,
A bird screeches down at Beahy Lake
As if she wants to say something
But cannot find the words.
All the worries and cares of yesterday finally fall asleep.
A cloud passes over the half-shut eye of the moon.

It is 4.30am.
Darkness steals away into the hedges,
Dawn comes down the fields like spilt milk.
A crucifix of light comes through the branches,
The geraniums on the window sill start to redden.
Morning begins, as if the trees have forgotten everything
And need daylight to call them by their names:
Beech, Ash, Sycamore, Hawthorn, Maple…
The moon is slow to disappear,
The purr of traffic on the bypass grows louder,
All life seems to curve in a roundabout way.

Catalogue Of My Room

I am a seascape painting, tilting to the right,
Pulling and dragging at the blue ceiling
And the white walls with the African carvings.

I am the white marble mantelpiece full of knick-knacks:
Sculpted candles, the Black Madonna of Montserrat, my aged father's
Photo, a screw driver, a sea shell, a piece of rock from Mount Etna.

I am the white shelves, full of books all about the
Walls,
The unsung painting of a tree with a rosary wrapped about its
Branches,
The sculpted straw hat for a mummer, a mask from a theatre
Persona.

I am a bust of Sophocles, with his head bashed
In,
A photo of myself in New York in the 70s.,
Tapes of the great composers: Mozart, Chopin, Beethoven,
A few of Bob Dylan,
My mother's prayer book, the green catechism, Uncle Frank's
Rituale in usum Cleri Hibernici.

I am the framed posters for: The Glass Menagerie, Oedipus Rex, Half
A Vegetable, Mother Courage and Her Children,
The cupped hands sculpture above Louis Macneice's selected
Poetry,
The pine shutter waiting to be hung, the framed photo of Noel Brown's
Funeral, with its face to the wall.

I am the echoes and whispers in this room,
I am the early riser at my desk,
I am now in this room and all that matters
Is the blank page before me.

Bellavally Gap

Between Legnaderk
And Altnadarragh
Sahara of white grass
And rusty rushes
Two homeless jackdaws
Beak to beak
On an electric wire,
Not a chimney in sight.

Feast Of Asses

I come across a pace of asses gathered together
In a cemetery bordering Leitrim and Cavan.
One hesitates ... one is lying on his back
Feet skyward ... one brays, complaining about
God knows what ... one nods off, as if listening
To painful gossip ... another turns away.

Nine asses with that tired suffering look
That comes from eating grass in the local graveyard
And listening to the grief of the wind
Among the grey headstones.

Nine asses cast out of Ballinamore,
Flanks caked in muck,
Big nostrils quivering, all willing
To carry their cross in procession.

Nine asses like ghosts in grey raincoats
From the Feast of Asses in The Middle Ages,
Awaiting the final signal on the steps of the altar:
Ite, Missa est: ... Hee-Haw, Hee-Haw, Hee-Haw ...

Crom

The town is off her guard ... lets her hair down.
Crom and his Twelve Idol Businessmen
Sidle down Main Street, in yellow underwear, caterpillar footwear,
     Shuttle and clank ..... shuttle and clank.
Scattering all before them,
Striking buildings with hydraulic hammers ...
Impact breakers, mammoth wrecking balls ...
     Shuttle and clank ..... shuttle and clank.
Building prisons, banks, madhouses ...
Schools of Technology, Institutes for concrete reasoning,
Enough to petrify the young into bricks in the wall.
     Shuttle and clank ..... shuttle and clank.
Crom and his Twelve Idol Businessmen build
House-boxes for us all, on the backsides of drumlins,
Beneath dolmens, beside the lakes, on the edge of river banks.
     Shuttle and clank ..... shuttle and clank.
Crom and his Twelve Idol Businessmen bop
To seismic music, night and day.
     Shuttle and clank ..... shuttle and clank.
Crom and his Twelve Idol Businessmen
Expect us all to fall before them,
     Shuttle and clank ..... shuttle and clank.
A modern version of an ancient myth,
It all depends on which side of the wall you fall,
     Shuttle and clank ..... shuttle and clank.

Catching Each Other By The Tail

What happens when banks collapse?
The walls fall out,
The roof caves in.

Will we leave the bed,
Risk dancing down the road?
Naked, in full view of the milkman, postman ...

Adrift on the New Roundabout,
Desperate to find our bearings,
Talking to ourselves and the rest of us,
Marching, striking, queuing ...
Listening to what RTE has to say,
All the Specialized and Proficient Talkers,
The cordon bleu of Banking
All confused but talking all the same.
Is there anybody home? Says I.

It's a whirligig, says Somebody.
Asylum seekers, refugees, immigrants
Hide behind half-doors, fridge doors,
Glass doors, cage doors, any door
As long as they get in
But now they can't get out fast enough
And heaven's door slams shut
Like the surge suppressor
On a computer.

A judge in a District Court
Sends a man to jail for whispering.
Bishops in buskins and zucchettos
Don't agree on Child Protection.
Politicians in mohair suits,
Grease the wheels of the treadmill,

Bend the Green Greenness of Éire
So the peas can run freely in their pods,
Then pause and listen to themselves.

All back to where we started,
Catching up with ourselves,
Round and round the merry-go-round
Catching each other by the tail.

Marrakech

A stork nests on top of a minaret, Berber houses
Wedge into the mountainside, jujube bushes ...
Goats climbing in the argan trees.

We are an inward people says the tour guide Ali Ben,
Riad, our internal garden, is surrounded by walls.

Winding streets tangle, array of goods in alleyways:
Barbouches, mokkala guns, semolina eyes, saffron, mint tea ...
Tiny henna stars glitter on a young girl's fingers.

We are an inward-looking people,
Intone the same chants at regular intervals
Beat out rhythms on bendir drums.

Women in burqas talk on mobile phones,
A young man, with a newly purchased satellite-dish
Between his legs, prays outside the mosque.

We are an inward people says the tour guide Ali Ben
Riad, our internal garden, is surrounded by walls.

Geometric motifs to lift your eyes from ceramic tiles,
Past plaster designs to cedar carvings,
Symmetry is a central feature in everything we do.

We are an inward-looking people,
Intone the same chants at regular intervals
Beat out rhythms on bendir drums.

Djemma El Fna Square is round the bend: musicians, snake-charmers,
Tooth-pullers, water-sellers ... Harira, tagine and couscous smells,
A man sleeps in the shade, unmoved by everything.

We are an inward people says the tour guide Ali Ben
Riad, our internal garden, is surrounded by walls.

We own kasbahs by the dozens, have cats in kaftans and jellabas
Underneath chairs and tables of every restaurant and café,
Look at the old man reciting the Koran from a trailer.

We are an inward-looking people,
Intone the same chants at regular intervals
Beat out rhythms on bendir drums.

We turn our cruciferous faces away from Mecca
To face our own gardens: Eden and Gethsemane
While Ali Ben continues with his mantra

We are an inward people
Riad, our internal garden, is surrounded by walls.

For Billy, Kathleen And Family

When words of sympathy are idle talk
We remember the lost words,
Wildly dancing on the lip of night.

Words beyond the turn for home,
Drift words, afraid to form a sentence,
Hooting words in the owl of winter light.

When words of sympathy are idle talk
We remember the unspoken
Wrapped in winter frost by a roadside.

Lichen words, clinging to stone and tree,
The bare feet of words running away from me
With the wind on their faces.

When words of sympathy are idle talk
We remember the inner words
That tear at the heart of God.

Words hiding in the wardrobe with our clothes,
A line of words like trophies on a mantelpiece,
Dream words, tucked away under the blanket.

When words of sympathy are idle talk
We remember the unspoken words
That keep coming home.

Olive Blossom

An olive blossom draws me in.
Tiny carnelian eyes
Ignite the four petals,
A cruciform
Lonely for prayer,
Thirsting for words.

November Moon

The moon is a golden head of curls
Hiding behind a bare tree,
Its furrowed forehead is full of worry,
Its drowned face below a sea of stars
Has yesterday's light on its lips.

December Evening

Response to painting by Pádraig Lynch

I come across the white grief of a field gate
Tied to the gloom of pallet and boards,
Swaddled bushes lie everywhere
Snow-green, snow-grey, snow-brown ...
Trees, dusty white, stretch like ghosts,
Shadows of clouds walk about the fields,
You can almost hear the hum of snow
Settling in for the long sleep.

Curve Of The Moon

Watch for her shadow
Behind the clouds,
Cradle of light in her arms,
Maiden, mother and moon,
Ladleful of milk in the stars
Hushed melody
                    Of winter snow.

The Music Of Snow

At first we hear
The faintest music of snow.
Then the moon slowly rises
And dreams us back
To childhood memories

Of cows chewing their cud
In the byre, a blackbird's alarm call
Across the hedges as darkness falls,
The eerie creak of the yard-gate
       In December wind swings back

To a first Christmas night
And we journey there,
Retracing our footprints in the snow
….. hurrying down lanes and country roads
To Midnight Mass.

The chapel opens its door,
A flicker of carol singing
Stirs into the light of words:
Glory to God in the highest
And peace to His people on earth.

2

Beyond The Wind

Beyond The Wind

Centenary celebration poem to Patrick Kavanagh, 2004

I can imagine him looking over
A fieldgate, knowing the hour had arrived,
Wondering why everyone deserted him,
Girls fell in love with the man in the moon.
The mirror of a pothole points a finger
To Inniskeen and to Golgatha ...
The drama of fields hurries to an end,
Scourged by briars, hiding from the neighbours,
He feared the hosanna crowd on the hill,
Known to shout "Hail"... "Crucify" with one breath,
Tired of the drop of mother's milk from the ponger,
He saw another cup beyond the wind,
Happy to be alone with himself
And to drink the silence and the dream.

Boochalawn Buí

The wild bee tosses my yellow hair where
I reside along a closed railway line
Since government surveys mapped my decline.
From that day forward, pain was always near
Living as I do in mist, fog and fear.
Staggerweed, stammerwort, names from outside
With their intended power to deride
Can't rob me of pollen and nectar here.
I love the risk, pleasure of the abyss
I am the shomeer come out of darkness,
Forsaken, I close my daisy yellow eye
On the grey incontinent Irish sky.
Whisper my name whenever you need me
Boochalawn, Boochalawn, Boochalawn Buí.[*]

* Hiberno-English for Ragwort.

Visiting Kierkegaard's Grave

A sense of doom hovers about your name,
Kierkegaard, a Danish word for churchyard,
Aloof in childhood, burdened by sorrow,
Frightened by an Old Testament God
That hooked you to the nails on the cross.
You searched inside your soul for months, years…
Discovered a new song, a leap in the dark,
A call to take chances, to walk alone.
A call that now drives me away from the crowd
To walk sidewalk after sidewalk, past kirks, canals …
And stand at your graveside in Copenhagen.
Time holds you darkly in this secret place,
Hidden in trees, covered in October leaves,
Kierkegaard, at one with your name at last.

Drama Festival

We become trees, lost to a forest of chairs
In the Town Hall. Snow covers our world.
Oedipus enters upstage centre,
Plants strange forgotten words along our paths.
We become rooted in clay at the crossroads,
Stars peep through darkness to speak to the snow,
The light of the moon passes through our branches,
Our leaves are full of the wind's chorus.
For a moment we have forgotten who we are.
Our Sunday hearts drink another blood,
A family tree creaks at its roots: Father, Mother,
Son and Daughter can never be the same again.
The adjudicator calculates in his head,
A practice old as Sophocles. Everyone waits.

Buskins In The County Museum

When bells clanged and chapel organ sang
In *Gaudio Magno*, his buskin boots
In marigold yellow, cherry red studs,
Waltzed below his crosier and altar skirts
In a slow liturgical procession.
And people who felt they walked in darkness,
Saw heavenly sole shimmers ascend
From the Pontifical Abbot's high-heeled boots.
Years later, the same boots, now footless,
Glare out at me from a glass cage
In the County Museum, smug and silent,
An exhibit for all to stare and wonder at
And a chilled thought flashes across my mind,
I once stooped low to lace them on his feet.

Gathering Mushrooms

We climbed into Tully's field, the gate rattled,
Sheep scattered, cows stood their ground as we strolled
Around in the hope of finding mushrooms.
You're blind as bats, Madge Reilly said,
I can see them sleeping under bedstraw
Hear them whispering in their dreams,
Her black thumb quenching the stars in the grass,
Their frail pink gills breathing a final tune.
Nightfall, the road lit up with the sparks
Of mushrooms beaming from bucket and hand,
Like pilgrims returning from the Holy Land,
Thraneens laden, beads dangling in the dark,
A glimmer from lost fields I long to find
Hidden somewhere in the back of my mind.

NOTE: Thraneens is a Hiberno-English word meaning: long
wisps of grass.

The Separator

We stood around the dairy floor, eyeing
All the gewgaws that were spread about:
Flying saucers, cans, crockery and spout,
Disc-fitting-into-disc, compressed in-between.
Our mother bent over the green machine,
Made it yowl and purr and sing,
While a stray cat on the sill looked in
At us, waiting patiently for the cream.
At first, the blue skim-milk gushed forward,
Then cream trickled, falling into circles.
Our pongers* reached out to intercept
The flow of something longed for, well timed.
It was singled out, homemade special cream,
Its inner nourishment continues to stream.

* Ponger: Hiberno-English, a metal mug.

To See September
Through A First Year's Eyes

For Brendan McCann

To see September through a first year's eyes
Amid shifting tides of maroon laughter,
Hear her fears, cherish the hopes of a youngster
As she explains her burning issues: *There's a bee*
Humming in the window of St. Jude's ...
One by one, they talk with him as with a friend,
Given pride of place on the road between two places.
The school-bell rings, the evening star shines
Through the office window and he knows it's time
To wipe the blackboard clean and dream,
Time to wait for the silence to whisper,
Time to move on and not look back,
Time to hear a thousand soft nibs write thank you
On a Loreto sea of wine.

The Child Lives Forever Deep Within Us

A celebratory poem
To mark 75 years of Loreto College Cavan

The child lives forever deep within us
And once in a while, that child laughs, cries …
Even sings with memories of school days
When thoughts were quavers away from a song,
Whispering down corridors in the night,
Long silence in study, our hearts beating
To the rhythms of the classroom, the exam clock
Ticking on to a hundred white faces.
Here in Loreto College Cavan, where drumlins
Are brooding since the Ice Age, nuns and teachers
With minds deep as a well, are quenching our thirst
And reminding us we're young talented people,
Deserving of love and exhorting us
Never to lose sight of the child within us.

Epithalamium

for Síodhna and Kevin

The chance of a couple meeting
Is filled with wonder, like leaves touching
In a breath of wind. As children, Síodhna and Kevin
Were central to their worlds in Cavan and Galway,
Blowing out candles on birthdays, making wishes
And dreaming, always dreaming of some special day.
All eyes are turned on Síodhna and Kevin today.
Rows of relations and friends in hats and best suits
Are gathered, confetti of conversations,
Candles burn on the altar, gifts are offered,
Bells ring out *Sanctus*, lips utter: "I Do".
For this is the flesh and blood of their promises,
The love that grows not only in words
But in the silences between words.

Postojina Cave, Slovenia

(Home to the Human Fish – Proteus Anguinus)

We were shuttled in train loads underground,
Past drapery of rock, lichen grey candles,
To a high altar in the underworld.
Eternal dripping, metronome of drops,
A flowering of water into stone,
Where skeletons of the unknown wrap
Their bones about a calcium organ.
An afterlife of rain bearing witness
To a human fish, lost in a tabernacle
Underground, rarity and wonder to us all.
Three fingers, two toes, ghostly white and blind,
Lost soul, smelling of damp, clawing its way
Along grit and sand into our dream world,
Where altars take root under the weight of darkness.

The Calf-Bearer

It wasn't the fore-locks of the marble horse
Or the ringlets of Kore that caught my eyes
But the calm and stare of the Calf-Bearer,
In the museum of the Acropolis.
A farmer like my father with a calf
Slung over his shoulder, the field his altar.
He knows the agony of clay, the language
Of weather, blaze of the sun, squally winds,
Apples dropping on the lap of autumn,
Winter under the trees of the moon.
Travelling alone, down the mountain side,
At one with the secrets of stone and clay,
Eyes set on the road ahead, never looking back,
The house always somewhere in the distance.

Talking To My Shadow

When will you dig me up? Get me out of here.
Rain water sings in my boots, the wind screams
Inside my head. I am smothered under
Bundles of sticks and fallen branches.
My weather-bitten face is the colour of clay,
My fingers, rods of winter ash, eyelids full
Of frozen tears. I am tired of leafy pillows
And the straw bed of this roadside ditch.
Listen to me, my loved one, you are more
Than what has happened to you, I will light
The dark ditch inside you; fire fills my mind.
Dipping my fingers in the dew of the night,
I will write love letters to the moon
On your behalf, soft as a baby's breath.

Cuilcagh

This woman is strange.
Perfume of moss and wild asphodel,
Squatting here in the wilderness,
Blanket of bog about her shoulders
Her fierce breasts held in place
By whins and heather.
Sheep graze on her,
Birds wing across her limbs,
The wind gives her words,
The sun lights up her chalky face.
Farmers drive stakes through her peaty flesh,
Black streams are veins
Winding slowly round her hips,
Bog water trickles down her legs.

Etna

From afar, you can smell her smoky breath,
Her jagged complexion cuts into the sky,
Smoke plumes rise above her head. She throws
Tantrums, wriggling red-hot spaghetti through
Her teeth, sending rocks flying down to sea.
Etna Mongibello will take your breath,
Divine and fierce, pines wither in her gaze,
Warp and woof of snow cover her fiery breasts.
Forever a fashionable lady,
She loves to model her almond stockings,
Chestnut shoes. Irresistible as ever,
In the amber and pink of her sunset,
I see the ghost of Empedocles walk
Around her lips to sup at her long tongue.

Sheela Na Gig

Call me Sheela, Baubo or Magdalene,
You'll find my image in remote places,
Hiding in ivy ruins of churchyards,
Reduced of late to leaves on Valentine Cards,
Resolved to stand firm. Call me day or night,
My mobile number is your invite.
You won't find me lacking, legs spread apart,
I'll lick your wounds, stitch your leaking heart.
I am that inner voice, once conversant
With monks on their way to silent prayer,
Gaping vulva in the curve of the moon,
Witch in the wind crooning a graveyard tune,
I howl across the flood fields of your dreams
To open grassy meadows in the sun.

Scarecrow Woman

I catch sight of her on a sea of wheat
Drifting past. Her blouse, jumper and skirt
Clamped to her bones with clothes-pegs,
Her face veiled in old straining-cloth,
A Sunday hat one side of her head,
Alone in the field with her secrets,
A black diamond stitched to her sleeve
To remind us of winter and her dead daughter.
Perched on a wooden leg on golden grain,
She sways to scare the crows away,
Drinks rain, breathes the wind,
A sprinkle of poppies ignites the ripples,
Her promise always, the gift of grain
And the hope of tomorrow.

Summer Holiday

We are a possessive people, attached
To small holdings, a view we take on trips
To staked out terraces on sandy strips.
Here we cultivate the sun's rays, dispatched
Beneath umbrellas, overtly mismatched:
Rosy pinks, tomato reds, pale parsnips.
We stretch to oil our navels, wet our lips,
Lost to holidays and feeling detached.
Here we sense the need to look out to sea,
To project ourselves onto a grotto
Of sea rock, the hills and the olive tree,
Holiday homes if we won the lotto,
Bemused by a side-show from a sand flea,
Drifting with the evensong of the sea.

Primal Loss

For John Montague on his 80th birthday

The loss of the first love of your life
Left you clasping at the blankets of sleep,
Your heart tugging to free itself, dreaming
Of a mother's smile that failed to show her face.
You took grief for a walk about the fields
Of Garvaghey, straying past the *Dolmens*
Of Childhood, determined to put your point across.
All roads lead to that primal loss.
You stopped looking in the same direction
As everyone else, mapped a new projection,
Few signposts, you learned the language of verse,
Shaped poems from stones in *The Rough Field*,
Found the locket your mother wore, revealing
A photo of a boy with curls in Brooklyn.

Evening Prayer

(at the grave of Robin Marsh)

Sunset is a curtain of fire this evening.
Snow is on the hills, the wheel that turns
The wind girdles your grave with leaves, as you lie
 Close to the doorway of Armagh Cathedral
Your high ground, at one with the symphony of souls.
I stand this December evening with a great sense of loss,
Searching for prayer words beneath a chestnut tree
At your graveside, adorned with holly wreathes,
A garland of white roses.
                              You sleep now in the cradle
Of the moon and roads cross and draw me back
To summer schools about that old shadowy Carleton
And the two Johns you loved to read: Montague and Hewitt
Are honey-cakes, sparks of stars to light you on your way.

3

Dánta i nGaeilge agus Aistriúcháin
Poems in Irish and Translations

Bealtaine

Is leanbh í an aimsir
Ag súgradh liom faoin spéir,
Cam an ime, solas gréine
An ghaoth ag séideadh
Gúna buí an aitinn,
Is caisear bhán mar gealach ar strae
Is rún na gcloch sa chré.

The Month Of May

The month of May is the child in me
Playing outside.
Buttercups are full of the sun,
The wind lifts the yellow dress
Of a whin bush for fun
And the dandelion is like
A moon that lost her way
And the stones have secrets
Buried in clay.

Maithiúnas Na bPeacaí

Tabhair maithiúnas
Do Bhean Uí Nualláin
A chaith uisce beirithe
Ar na Jehovah Witnesses
Is iad á míniú a gcreideamh
Ag doras a tí.

Tabhair maithiúnas
Don tSiúr Máire na nAingeal
A chuir hata donsa ar dhaltaí,
Iad a thaispeáint do cách,
Iad a tharraingt mórthimpeall na scoile,
Is an slua beag ag magadh fúthu.

Tabhair maithiúnas
Do Phearla Ní Cheallaigh
A chuir mallacht orm
Nuair a d'inis mé di
Go raibh cúig phónaí suas an bhóthair
In ionad cúig asal.

Tabhair maithiúnas
Don chrochadóir Ó Dálaigh a dhíol Woodbines dom:
Deich bpingin ceann amháin,
'Sé ag síor leagadh na mallachtaí orm
Nuair nach raibheas ag tarraingt an deataigh
Síos go hionga na gcos.

Tabhair maithiúnas
D'amadáinín *Poker*
A thóg a bhod amach faoin mbínse
I rang a sé, crom ar a chuid oibre,
Greim ar fhorcraiceann, ní raibh cosc le cur air,
Ag péinteáil a bhodín le dúch dubh.

Forgiveness Of Sins

Grant forgiveness
To Mrs. Nolan for throwing scalding water
On the Jehovah Witnesses
And they only explaining their faith
On her door step.

Grant forgiveness
To Sr. Mary of the Angels
Who put a dunce's hat on scholars
And took them from class to class
For all to see, scoff and jeer.

Grant Forgiveness
To Pearl Kelly who cursed me
When I told her
There were five ponies up the road
Instead of five asses.

Grant forgiveness
To the hangman Daly who sold me Woodbines
At ten pence each and he forever cursing me
When I wasn't inhaling them
Right down to my toe nails.

Grant forgiveness
To that little *eejit* " Poker", who took his bodín out
From under the desk in 6th class, no stopping him,
Bent on pulling his foreskin back
Painting his bodín with black ink.

Ciaróg Dhubh

Bhí na ballaí ag éisteach linn
Oíche amháin a chasadh orm é,
Blaincéad dhubh ar a dhroim
Ag taisteal faoi scáth na hoíche
San dorchadas chiúin.
Duine den teaglach
A théann i bhfad siar.

Dia duit, A Chiaróg
Bhí tú ann romhainn
Gan bheith ró chraiceáilte
Cé go n-itheann tú gach ní,
Taos fiacla, gliú, bun toitíní …
Is tá sé ráite go maireann tú
Gan do cheann ar feadh seachtaine,
'S is féidir leat tú féin a choscaint
Ó radaíocht núicléach.

In dúirt an chiaróg liom:
Bí ciúin,
Mairim san spás idir na bhfocal.

Cockroach

The walls were listening to us
One night I bumped into him,
A black blanket over his shoulders
Travelling in the black silence
Of disguise by night.
One of the household
That goes a long way back.

Hello Cockroach,
You were here before us
Although you weren't much crack,
Eating all around you,
Toothpaste, glue, cigarette butts,
And it's said that you can live
Without your head for a week
And that you can protect yourself
Against nuclear radiation.

And the cockroach said to me:
Be quiet,
I live in the space between words.

4

Diary Of A Town

A Dramatic Poem

Diary of a Town

I

They were all waiting for things to happen,
Dividing time between waking and dreaming.
Some lived in Ballalley Row, Porter Row, Waterlane …
You could say everyone was in the audience and no one on the stage.
When I look back
Shadows creep from nowhere,
Places and people come alive again:
The strange look of the trees at night,
The untaxed cars hiding in the backyards,
Old walls, byroads, the long and short division of fields,
Rain water on the Scrabby Road.
There's a cold wind coming in from Lough Sheelin
That sends a sea of grass up the hill.
And from the hilltop, fields and houses move with the clouds,
The Lady of The Rocks looks down on the town
With her limestone smile.
Slowly, night makes way for day.

The boys are tussling over a red ball in the school yard.
The master blows his whistle and they line up.
Fisty Finnan gets nought for sums,
Johnny Tucker's fingers are smeared with ink.
The sing song of tables and the drumming of catechism
Echo .....

| 6 | 1s | are 6 |
| 6 | 2s | are 12 ..... |

Is the Father God?
> *The Father is God and the first person of the Blessed Trinity.*

Is the Son God?
> *The Son is God and the second person of the Blessed Trinity.*

Is the Holy Ghost God?
The Holy Ghost is God and the third person of the Blessed Trinity.

Johnnie Kelly wipes his nose on his sleeve.

The *glantóir**** goes missing and Fisty Finnan gets six slaps on the hand.
Another half hour of nib dipping and out to play.

Donnelly's Bus trundles down Main Street, heading for Somewhere,
Johnny Matt comes from the Barrack Spout
With two buckets of water in a box-barrow, dripping and spilling …
Three girls sitting on the steps of the hotel chant their gibe:

> *Johnny Matt skinned a goat and threw the fat on the fire.*
> *Men, women, dog and cat*
> *Come out to talk to Johnny Matt*
> *Johnny Matt, Johnny Matt, Johnny Alleluia …*

January walks through the streets
Looking ahead and looking back.
Morning returns to find the night covered in snow.
A white cowl spreads across the rooftops,
Icicles hang from the gutters,
Rosset's cat is out crying in the snow for a Tom,
She whispers to the snow:

> *Meow …Meow … Meow …*
> *Any TomCat will do,*
> *We cats have no time for morals.*
> *Meow … Meow … Meow ….*

A blackbird skims across Main Street and up Waterlane,
A child throws a snowball at the snow,
The evergreens above the chapel are half white,
The first bell rings out.
Frosty eyes look up from the snow and sparkle,
A ghost tiptoes round the corner,
A few scattered people climb the hill and head for the chapel.

Is that the first or second bell for Mass?
Heads bowed at the altar rails,
Eyes shut, tongues hanging out for salvation,
Bald heads nod at women's hats and scarves.
Every Sunday the same,
Kneeling …standing …sitting …
Kneeling for a long time …sitting for a short while,
Shopping after Mass … shelves of tins:
Sardines, peas, beans … assortment of sweets, barley sugar,
Chester cakes in Doherty's window …blood oranges in from Sicily.
Light brown tissue paper to wrap the loaves in,
A ball of twine hangs from the ceiling
Awaiting the nimble fingers of T.P.
Sunday dozes into Monday
A crow leaves a branch in Burns' field,
Loops and flies the other way.

* Gaelic for duster.

II

February begins to lift its head.
Snowdrops nod in the wind.
Lonely farmhouses hear lambs bleating in the haggard.
The town listens to the laughter of children in the school yard:

> *Hop! Hop! My little horse*
> *Hop! Hop Again!*
> *How many miles to Dublin?*
> *Three score and ten*
> *Will I be there by candle light?*
> *Yes! Yes! And back again*
> *Hop! Hop! My little horse*
> *Hop! Hop Again!*

Mickey Rourke straightens the handlebars of his moustache,
Three girls sitting on the steps of the Greville Arms, chew gum
And enquire:

> *Did ye get a Valentine, Mickey?*
> *Did ye get yer candle blessed, Mickey?*
> *Did ye get yer throat blessed, Mickey?*
> *Did she make ye a Bridget's Cross, Mickey?*

Mickey grunts.
Cock Fagan is spreading dung in Tully's field,
He stops to light a fag butt
On the zip-fork of his blue jeans,
Complete with sideburns, Brylcream glistening in the February sun,
He talks and sings to the mule and a cart full of dung:

> *I want to be a teddy boy and sing like Lonny Donnegan:*

> > *Oh! My old man's a dustman*
> > *He wears a dustman's hat*
> > *He wears Cor-Blimey trousers*
> > *And he lives in a council flat.*

Guard Cooney stands to attention at the corner.
The dough is rising in Pat The Baker's.
Martin Ruther, cap with flaps down round his ears, is out with the bucket.
The guards' wives gossip:

> *What's that fella doing with the rabbit's ears?*
> > *Collecting slops for a slip of a sow.*
> *Did you hear Sheila Mac is marrying a monkey from Kilcogy?*
> > *Never. The poor gorilla.*
> *I'm killt with the chilblains.*
> > *I told you what to do,*
> > *Soak them in your wee and they'll disappear overnight.*

Someone is out polishing the brass on the door of The Ulster Bank.
Busty Mahety, fireman and painter,
Wets the bed in a fit of false awakening
> *Ay! Jasus! Not again …*
He has a thick slice of loaf for breakfast,
Then leans across the wall for the rest of the day,
Waiting for a house to go on fire.
Nurse Doyle, complete with Gladstone Case,
Goes to pull a rabbit from its burrow.
Midwife most merciful,
Friend to mothers far gone,
Mothers in teems of sweat.
Mrs. Chat Dooley sells herrings and whiting from a pick-up truck on Friday,
Boxes of herrings… haddock, cauliflowers, tomatoes…
Onions in net bags. Mrs. Chat Dooley guts the fish while you wait.
School children gather round the truck,
Stick their fingers in the open mouths of herrings
And feel the prickle of their glassy teeth.

> *Hello! Hello! Hello,* says old Dooley,
> *A good day it is, indeed it is a good day*
> *A good day it is* ….. Then looking up at the sky he informs all:
> *It may come to rain yet; I feel it in my bones.*
> *There you are; now you have it.*

Three o'clock, all the funeral bells ring out.
White alb, purple stole of the priest,
Mourners in black, up beside the coffin,
Small table, complete with white cloth cover for offerings,
The men file past in single line,
Jingle of half crowns.
Brass bucket with holy water ...hyssop-stick,
A sprinkling of holy water on the coffin:

> *Kyrie eleison, Christe eleison,*
> *Pater noster .....*
> *Et ne nos inducas in tentationem*
> *Sed libera nos a malo...*

Four brothers shoulder the coffin,
Down the long lane to Granardkille .
The glut of graves is privy to whispered conversations:
> *She was taken bad a year ago; took her time about dying,*
> *We all get there in the end...*
> > *We do indeed...*

Thud of clay on the coffin,
Open grave to inner darkness.

Jack Traynor, hairy nostriled and doubled chinned
Stands to attention at the butcher's-block.
Liver, kidneys, steak, strings of sausages, ox tails, cow's tongue,
Bullock's hearts, Lamb shoulder and lamb shank .....
Chipping and chopping away. Skewers and scrapers, saws and cleavers ...
Knives sing on sharpening steel; the bench is streaked in blood.
Sheets of grease proof paper to one side, sawdust on the floor,
Three sheep hang from meat hooks,
There's a poster for a carnival in Mullahoran behind a haunch of beef.
Mrs. Keenan, banker's wife prim and proper, parks her bicycle on the street.

> *Good morning Jack, two gigot chops, – cut away the fat, Please,*
> *And bones for the dog.*

She counts out pennies, thrupenny bits, tanners
And places them in the maw of his big hand.
 Jack yawns and dreams of loins and genitals
And 150 naked women running wild
Outside the Granada Ballroom.

A given time. A given place.
Every townland has a ghost or two looking at the past.
The fields dream of seeds given back to clay.
The crows fly from the trees in Burns' field,
A calf jumps out of the well at Tober Gowna,
Runs down the hill and the water after him. So the old
people say…
Ghosts minding their own business at this unearthly hour,
Hear the commotion
Of the yes and the no
Of the now and evermore:
      552AD. There was a sickness called the Sawthrust
      There was much frost and wind in 588AD.
      The virgin Sawhyn, from Clonbroney, dead since 736AD.
      Fiachra, from Granard, died 765AD.
So the Annals say.
A burnt patch by the roadside is observed
By the single eye of a raindrop.

Old mother moon is coming out
Over the barley hill,
Over the awful silence of fields,
Minutes are nibbling away at the light,
Crows come home to roost
Like black snow crossing the hills.
Tonight everywhere and everything is waiting
For something to happen.
Helen Sheridan, fifteen years old, talks in her sleep
And walks across a lake with cowslips and amaranths in her hair.

Cluckcluck …cluckcluck…cluckcluck …..
Joe O'Reilly hears horses trotting in his sleep,
Mary Verdon drops her teeth into a glass of water by the bedside.
Listen:
> *What's that noise in the attic? …in the kitchen? … on the stairs?*
> *Houses and rooms have secrets.*

Hughie Small, Busty Mahety and The Danger Smith
Are swilling pints of porter in The Star Bar.
Hughie counts the rows of bottles on the shelf
8…9…10…11…. Busty drinks to escape a medical condition,
And The Danger Smith, unable to raise his life,
Rows with his nose in the mirror,
The barman, standing in the way of the door, shouts:
> *Have you any homes to go to?*

Pearl Waters, with the red lipstick,
Lets her hair down and leads the town into temptation.
Piston and cylinder throbbing
In Fiat 127s, Triumphs and Mini Minors,
Corset on the chair, garters on the floor,
One transparent night, pulling … dragging,
Up and over,
Dog jumps bitch, stallion mounts mare,
Billy on the nanny,
Creaking bed-frame,
Pearl thighs, red toe-nails, Pearl curls,
Pearl loves to be touched,
Pearl ellipse, Pearl curve, all pink Pearl
All wild and plotting Pearl,
Pearl in heat,
Mons Veneris …Hilltown of Venus,
Lean forward milky Pearl
Pearl about to take a bath
And the whole town gawking at her.
Pearl was once as white as snow
Many many blue moons ago.

The two shilling rows in the Odeon Cinema
Have cushioned seats,
The curtain opens to applause and cheer,
HIT THE DECK ...Jane Powell, Debbie Reynolds, Ann Miller,
Luscious showgirls ...musical spectacular,
Usher in the aisle with his torch and peak-cap,
Separates the lovers,
Seventy four mouths munch crisps, slug Fanta and Coke,
Eyes glued to the screen,
Coming soon:
BY THE LIGHT OF THE SILVERY MOON,
With Doris Day and Gordon MacRae.

Janey Early takes to the streets to settle her nerves,
Past Donohue's Corner, up the hill, counting the steps,
Past the Celtic Cross on the left
To the lonesome church, the big iron bell,
In for a few prayers, a short visitation:
> *Lord help me stop crying,*
Out the chapel gate and up the laneway to the Virgin Grotto,
Wailing evergreens, jagged rocks:
> *O Mary conceived without sin*
> *Pray for us who have recourse...*
Down the other hill, lines of drills
In the back gardens of O'Callaghan Terrace,
Janey, dotty on Aspirins, and other medications, talks to herself:
> *I'm taking red pills for me blood pressure,*
> *And blue ones and yellow ones to make me sleep.*
Down New Road, a blast of wind and rain,
Corner boys, at the Market House, jibe and whistle:
> *How are ya fixed for tonight Janey?*
Janey journeys on, past the porter barrels outside King's,
Past Morrissey's, Leahy's Chemist, McGahern's Garage,
Heading for the convent, heading out, heading beyond,
Talking to herself ... to the dying ... and the dead ...
> *Mick the poor man fell into a threshing machine ...*
> *Mary was taken away in an ambulance because she had bad dreams,*
> *Lord help us all...*

Ash Wednesday.
There's a long line waiting for ashes in the chapel,
All waiting to be marked:

> *Memento homo,quia pulvis es,*
> *Et in pulverem reverteris.*

A reminder in Latin of our mystical ending
To all those who have been eating sin for supper.

III

March wind makes us shiver,
Its hoarse voice is heard in every throat,
Its breath is sharp, its ancient words cut stone,
It scorches grass; it burns the flush of flowers,
Dead shamrock on a button hole,
Singed overcoat of wool on barbed wire,
It roars down Market Street and Barrack Street,
It shouts underneath the slates of every house
And fills us full of fear of losing one another.
  Boom. —Boom.—BoomBoom.—BoomBoom.—Boom.—BoomBoom .....
The time signal on the radio ...O'Donnell Abú
Is blaring from the two Miss Bradys' hovel.
A large dwelling house and Paper Shop in sad neglect.
Never a sunrise or a sunset let inside,
Boarded windows, unwise virgins, tired of measuring
Day and night, they live in candle light.
Webs and dust everywhere, hills and mountains of newspapers,
Tabby cats, black cats, Manx cats ...
Some are taking a nap; some are sipping milk from saucers,
More meowing, an old mangy buck is nibbling something small
In a corner. Cats' piss everywhere.
Two ragged ladies behind the counter,
Raw scalps under headscarves, hairs on their chins,
Their awful white faces in the flicker of candles,
Tracks of their wormy fingers in a loaf of bread.
A half empty bottle of milk on the counter.
Women determined to bring news of the outside world
To us all, selling *The Irish Times, The Independent* and *Press*.

Good Morning birdsong daisy dawn.
A hundred different alarm clocks go off,
First squeals from babies for bottles.
Crackle of radio ...early morning news.
Clattering buckets, milk bottles rattling.
One morning resembles another and sleep lingers.

They all hate to leave the warm bed.
Cold bare feet on the bathroom floor,
Half-shut eyes looking into mirrors.
Mouth washing, shaving, combing,
Brushing away the fears of the night,
All in a hurry to face the earthly morning.
Mrs. Farrelly throws a splash of pink paraffin in the range to light the fire,
Spits on the hot plate to see her spittle dance,
Then puts the kettle on.
Jack Hall, postman is on his rounds.
A few women head up the hill to Mass and pray with their heads in
    their hands
And thank God for another day.

Mick Mulligan brings out bicycles
And places them against the wall of his repair shop on Moxham Street.
Widow Reilly's only lovely daughter, Margaret Mary,
Tells to the morning star her tale
Of having to wear canary yellow stockings for her mother's sake.
Dan Doyle beats hell out of the ass up Dagger's Hill,
        Go on you lazy fucker…go on you lazy fucker.
Parks the cart by the roadside,
Ties the ass to a stump of a whitethorn bush
And leaves the ass and his fragile daughter Bridgie there all day,
While he squanders the hours away with Jimmy Fay.
Dan the Piper is going to a football match or coming home.
Mary Verdon, No. 3, Waterlane, comes to the door:
        I had the bleeding last night,
        Me varicose veins are rising
        And me gallstones are paining me.
            You're a living martyr Mary,
            That's what everyone says.

Mary Green shares the sweets of sin with Dirty Jimmy up against a wall.
The poor priest and canon can't make saints of them all.
The bell rings,
And Mary and Jimmy can't tell the ding from the dong.

Lines of houses all the same,
Ball Alley Row and Water Lane,
The wind coming under the door,
Patterned lino on the floor,
Damp inscriptions on the walls
Curl of fly paper hanging in the halls,
Holy pictures and TV,
There's little more to see.

Out on the street, children are playing
Hula Hoop and skipping rope,
Tee-hee girls draw chalk-boxes on the toe-path,
Hop-scotching on one leg, boisterous boys shout:
    Dolly has a potty under her bed.
Ring A Ring A Rosy Girls
Gather primroses, cowslips in Durken's field,
One girl stays at home by herself:
    I sat on the hill
    And cried my fill
    And drank my ponger of milk

Brave boys climb in the high branches to the crow's nest,
Older boys dream
Of Peggy's leg that never wore a garter.
More read *The Beano* and *The Dandy*,
Tell me a story before you go to bed.

I stay outside and dream for them.
I sing my song alone
And I listen at every turn of the road,
A bewildered heap of stones refuses to go away,
Fields climb the hills, footsteps walk in front of me.
Tree spirits talk:
    Remember us as we are…as it is,
Men bend over the drills in silence,
The wind is coming through a draughty gap
Sending a swathe of hay over on its back,

Rust red sheds behind the houses
Sing in the rain. Gortawillan Lane
Surrenders its secrets.

Teenage lovers cry unto the sky
Out of the long wet grass in Keegan's field,
Bad mouthing nuns and priests.
Leaning against a rock in the quarry,
Philomena's red dress reeks of perfume,
Des has a wild dance in his eyes,
Rising and settling,
Waxing and waning, intimate and repelling
Panting breath, flush on her face,
Philomena's lips part
Pear shaped tongue slips out,
Slips in again …
All Des sees is her injection mark,
No chance of a fall from grace this evening:
    No Des … No … No…I'm not doing it, maybe after The Intermediate.

Is that another bell ringing?
    Hailmaryholymary … Hailmaryholymary … Hailmaryholymary …..
We love our sins and our bad humours,
We love to ask for forgiveness,
We love to get the spots off our souls,
    Father forgive me for I don't know what I'm at.
We love to hang our heads like daffodils
And nod away in the wind
We love to kneel in black boxes
And mumble away at our sins:
Father I didn't fast.
    Father I said a wrong word.
    Father I met a girl behind a wall…
    Met her in a field …in a gripe
    In the hayshed…under a lorry…up a tree,
    Father I didn't know what I was doing.
    Father… Will there be sex in heaven?
    Hailmaryholymary … Hailmaryholymary … Hailmaryholymary …..

The Easter ceremonies
Bring nuns up from the convent
Like black and white bees from a hive
To swarm about the chapel gate.
A cold wind comes in from Siberia,
The grass by the roadside shivers,
Coughs ... colds ... flu ...
Everyone sneezing and snorting,
No bells on Good Friday –
Clip- clap- clip- clap of the clapper,
Purple drapery on statues, wrapped crucifix,
An entire town gathered to witness
Nails in the hands and feet,
Pascal light in the darkness,
A town suckled on grief and fed on tears
Ponders the hope of:
     Lumen Christi ... Deo Gratias.
Easter Sunday,
Life-Death-Life
White as new light,
The priest unlocks the tabernacle,
Slides the veil to one side
And takes the ciborium out,
Mona Lisas in Easter bonnets slide up the aisle,
Lent is over ——*Hosanna ... Hosanna ... Hosanna ...*
Easter eggs renew our appetites,
Tin cans lined in moss are full with
Hen eggs, duck eggs, goose eggs –
The whole town happily eating after the long fast.
Kitty Kiernan sends an Easter Egg and a hug to Michael.

IV

Golden April,
Blaze of whins, a blast of wind,
Bees venture out for a first look about.
There stands a hill not far from the town
That turns from green to brown.
Two Massey Fergusons are harrowing it to hell.
The men grow tired of the broken clay,
Abandon their tractors in the field
And compose this lay:

A Tall Tale

Or

The First Gravy Train Into Town

One sultry morning, once upon a time,
In the month of April,
The town was taking it easy,
When a hag from Trumra and a dog fox from Gallid
Hastened to the steps of The Greville Arms Hotel
For a better view of the parade,
Guard Moore and Guard Cooney were wearing plus fours.
The whole town was discussing the main function of the
    First Gravy Train.
The train arrived late for a start,
All the *Pater Nosters* were kneeling on the steps of the hotel,
Praying to St. Swithin,
The Rinn Roe Ceili Band struck up a tune,
A ghost of a late abbot from Abbeylara
Was carrying the bones of a local saint in a shoe box
And nobody passed much remarks on him.
The choir sang a polyphonic version of:
Pouring Rain, Weather That Storm and *Easter Snow.*
The two inseparable sisters, the Miss Bradys came to the door to peep.
The local politician, Councillor C. Rooster was crowing about the town's
Proud History and how two Sicilian brothers, Espresso and Cappuccino

Came to the town in the middle of the night
And changed the format of thinking.
They were great talkers and sat up the entire night
Talking about what they would do for the town they love so well.
Then the Canon, the Grand Old Inquisitor
Asked for silence and there was a great hush over the moat,
All along the streets and the footpaths
And the canon blessed The First Gravy Train:
    Bisto …Bisto … Sancto Bisto,
And he sprinkled it with Holy Water,
And the entire population shouted: *Amen.*

It is early
When birds sing in first light,
Dandelions open their golden eyes,
Wild strawberries stretch their limbs
And playful lambs find a safe place in the field
Where life is held together in a childlike way
If only for a day.
Fields are not mute you know,
They talk …Yes …The talking fields,
Trees speak, stones chatter, bushes wail
For the fields have stories:
Once upon a time
There was a world of clay and stone
And fish and stars
And children heard about a green lion,
A dog with three legs,
A necklace of heads, a girdle of hands
And an old hag's hut
Revolving on a chicken's foot.
And the stories strike back at those who try to change them.
And lone bushes are best left alone.

Back in the town
Mrs. Muldoon looks over her privet hedge
And asks the same questions of Jack Hall the postman every morning:

Busy day?… Who's getting letters?… Who's the parcel for?…
More clothes from America?… I suppose?
A blackbird builds her nest in the privet hedge,
A few stragglers are coming down the hill from Mass,
Further down the street Busty Mahety throws raw liver on the pan,
Turns away, coughs and spits into the coal bucket,
Martin Ruther is whipping the hell out of a spinning top on
　　Moxham Street,
He says he's too sick to be at school.
Each year on the first of April, the town's people
Offer the rosary for the women and men of Scrabby,
That their electricity won't be disconnected,
And that they may get themselves out of bed every morning
By pulling their own pigtails.

More April showers are promised on the forecast this morning.
A bellows breathes in Jimmy Flynn's forge,
He talks football, scores goals, kicks points
And is sent off for putting the wrong shoe on the wrong foot
Of a mule.

Winking stars appear …..
Little windows to our souls in darkness,
The town's voice quietens into the night,
Inner voices of the people sing to themselves in sleep.
Their voices rise above the chorus of the day,
Above the crowd, mob and congregation
They sing alone in sleep:
Mary Major screams internally,
Someone is walking inside her heart
And she feels the thud of his boots in her blood.
Mother Angela sprinkles children's tears about the playground.
Bogán Kiernan, retired commercial traveller,
Rides a bicycle through the roads and byways of his dreams,
Canon O'Kane, parish priest carries everyone's cross
Up the Main Street, up the hill, across a desert of ploughed land,
To a field of stones.

Mike The Barber looks into a big mirror
And shaves the dead face of every man in town.
Mary Verdon remembers her childhood
And cries all night beside the turnip pulper in the shed.
Mrs. Blaney writes messages to herself every day
And reads them aloud in her sleep:

> Dear Mrs. Blaney,
>   Remember to leave the key under the mat
>   Just in case Mr. Blaney returns unexpectedly from the grave,
>   And report the scoundrels of children
>   That knock and kick down your door,
>   To the master, the nuns, the priests and the guards.
>   And don't forget to boil the potatoes,
>   And pay for the milk and the bread
>   And God willing leave money for the priests
>   In case you die in your bed.
>   Yours truly,
>   May Blaney.

Another April morning arrives; the sun is about to rise,
Grim reds, dead black, flushes of vermilion,
A ghost comes down the old road
And vanishes with the fog.
First the pyx of the sun then the monstrance,
A breeze blows the darkness away,
Syllables of sunlight, spurts of rain,
Smudges of cloud across the curve of the moon,
Spring is looking out from under the trees in the park,
Wood-anemones, primroses, celandines open their eyes.
And life happens,
As it was in the beginning,
Is now and ever shall be,
A robin lifts a twig
And flies to build her nest,
It starts to rain again. Blue, red and green umbrellas walk to Mass,

The canon's wipers won't *swish swash*
And he drives up the hill, his head out the window.
Two dogs sniff each other in the rain,
Bow-wow… and pass on.
Rosset Kelly puts his hand into his raincoat pocket,
Takes out nothing and calls his manx cat in out of the rain:
>   *Pussypussy … pussypussy … wetpussy*
>   *Psh… psh … psh … psh…*

Rain is making music everywhere
Babble of showers, leaking gutters,
Cantabile of raindrops on slate and galvanised roofs,
Squelch of Wellingtons on the pavement,
Memory hovers about with the rain,
Flooding the corridors of our brain,
Makes noise in the gullies on Waterlane.
Men, women and children with mugs of tea
Hear the weather forecast and ponder the thought of a long wet day.
Cock Fegan can't stand the rain,
He takes out a picture of Elvis
And sings to it:
>   *Can't you see?*
>   *I love you, please don't break,*
>   *My heart in two.*
He stops abruptly to tell us:
>   *I'm off to Hollyhead in the morning,*
>   *You'll all drown in the town,*
>   *This town is truly Purgatory,*
>   *A place where people suffer*
>   *Before they take the boat to England.*
Old Dooley has wind of local gossip,
He walks the streets in the rain talking to everybody and nobody.
>   *Hellohellohello, Hellohellohello,*
With a grin on his face like a rat in a graveyard he ponders:
>   *Boys Oh Boys!*
>   *The noodynaedy wan in the drapery,*
>   *Has to leave in a hurry,*

Proof of the pudding, bun in the oven,
Broth of a boy from the next parish,
So they're saying,
· *Mum's the word, mum's the word,*
Boys Oh boys,
In every sense and meaning.
Terrible rain, more promised,
The swallows will be late on arrival
Goodbye, goodbye, goodbye.

Canon O'Kane, alone in the presbytery,
Is sifting words for his next sermon:
A time to reap… a time to sow…
    Time falls in darkness.
    Time walks by your side,
    Slowly at first, then in a hurry,
    Time sleeps with you … time eats you…

Rosset Kelly plans to purchase:
    I'll get a new Raleigh bike
    On the never-never
    And cycle out to Bord na Móna
    Work in the bog for May
    Freewheeling down at the break of day
    I'll take comfort in the job
    A man of means …nut brown, stripped to the waist,
    I'll lunch outdoors with the best of them
    Busty Mahety , Danger Smith …
    We'll drink our flasks of tea, eat ham sandwiches
    And talk politics and religion
    And cycle home each evening to the sweetness
    Of well-earned sleep and dreams of Pearl's lips and her long wet hair.

V

Holy Mother month of May,
Rosy halo of first communion,
White goddess of the hawthorn flush,
Oaten cakes round and flat,
Primrose on cusp of thorn,
Pleroma of roses on the garden wall,
Mayfly on Lough Sheelin,
Innumerable voices rattle on:

> *I'll sing a hymn to Mary,*
> *The mother of my God,*
> *The Virgin of all virgins .....*

The nuns set up May Altars
To the young girls they once were,
Canon O'Kane of the woeful countenance
Leads the devotions:

> *Virgin most prudent ... Virgin most venerable ...*
> *Virgin most renowned ...*

Philomena laughs
All the way home from the chapel,
Des follows her up the road,
And they pair off into the field, beyond the gap,
Smell of wet clay,
Heading for the curve of the moon.
Scent of hawthorn blossom burns inside us all,
Maia mother of Mercury, hears the call
And Autumn unveils what's sown in Spring.

Two Redemptorists, black soutane and giant rosary
Arrive on a Mission of self-denial,
One walks up and down the chapel
For fear someone might fall asleep.
The other yells his sermon and jumps about the pulpit:

> *We are all fallen angels*

Trapped in our bodies
Barred in a ribcage till death
Our flesh, food for maggots and worms,
Our souls are meant for God,
All will be made clear to us when we die
And living is only about dying...and dying about living.

The Danger Smith with the grog-blossom on his nose
Sits up, listens and goes on the dry for a day or two.
Pearl asks God to keep her away from men.
Philomena prays for a secret intention,
Girls in black mantillas promise chastity before the altar,
Two stalls on either side of the chapel
Sell rosaries to beat the band: Bronze ones ...Silver ones ... Gold ones ...
Scapulars and *Agnus Deis* to wear next your skin.
Every sort of medals : miraculous ...St. Christopher ...St. Jude ...
Statues of The Sacred Heart ...The Blessed Virgin ...The Child of Prague
The whole town is coming down with Religion
But the Redemptorists leave for Tubbercurry
And the same old sins keep coming back.

Children from Moxham Street are playing bus with Children from
    Waterlane.
Mouthing engine noises:
Beeb Beeping up and down the footpath:
    VROOM——VROOM——VROOM——VROOM——
    VROOM——BEEP——BEEP. RIMM——RIMM——
    RIMM——RIMM
They soon grow tired of the game
And turn to insulting one another:
    Go home to your scabby spuds
    Your pigs' trotters and fried bread.
Waterlane replies:
    Fuck yis all in Moxham Street with your Tapioco Faces
    And your Semalina Arses from the senna pods on Saturday.
The verbal abuse continues into the night:
    Big head.
    Gawky.

Cowardly Cowardly Custard.
Go home to your stirabout
Fuck Off.
The first round of the B Division League
Has begun in Heslin's field.
Someone kicks the ball over the ditch,
Spectators lift their heads to watch the clouds gather.
And the two teams start kicking one another.
Danger Smith floors a fella with his fist.
The Ref is crawling about in the net.
Heslin's cows are eating shirts, trousers and braces
At the upper end of the field.
Ward's dog mounts another mongrel bitch behind the goals
The ball returns from the next field
The game resumes.

When the game is slack and there's no rowing
John Kelly turns to Jack and makes an observation:
Look at that for a line of crosses going up the fields, man.
I had a job once with the ESB when the country was going electric.
You could be put doing anything, man,
Pulling giant spools of wire through fields and gaps,
Digging holes for poles …tarring poles … climbing poles, man.
How did you get up the pole, John?
You stepped into the grips, man, clipped them to your boots,
Strapped yourself to the pole for fear you'd fall
And up you went
Lugging transformers up the poles for nineteen shillings a week, man,
Them transformers are the electric brains of the country
Fork lightning does away with them in a flash.

VI

Midsummer.
Noonday is heavy in this happy town.
Sun blinds down on shops,
The sparrows are silent,
Ward's dog is asleep on the footpath ,
Dorothy Doran sits in her wine red chair taking the sun.
Shopkeepers come to the doors to look at the heat
And watch the line of children come to Larry's Shop
For ice lollies...Mr. Freezes and vanilla cones.
Martin Ruther goes into Doherty's to buy a lucky bag.
Finds Tommy asleep behind the counter.
The shop is full of trays of buns with cream and icing,
Chester cakes, bun loaves full of currants,
Martin leaves Tommy to his sleep, forgets the lucky bag,
Fills his pockets with buns and heads down the street.

A bumblebee is beating its wings
Behind the blind in Mrs. Major's shop window,
Sheets of newspaper are yellowing in the summer heat,
Up the old road the council men are tarring,
Black rakes, black spraying cans, black hands, black faces.

Out for the day.
Donnelly's bus stops at Maggie Dick's for Anothertown.
A journey up and down,
Past bushy green hedges,
Humpty dumpty hills, scraggy stones,
Cocks of hay, bales of hay,
The bus driver leans over the steering wheel
And waits for passengers to come down the laneways:
> *The clocks are never together in this country,*
> *No sense of time... but they won't be late for their funerals,*
> *That's for sure ...old ways die slowly round here.*
Clamps of turf sleep in the bog, clouds roll by,
Fieldgates, yardgates, going to rust,

All houses great and small,
Roses in the gardens,
Trees and bushes to break the force of the wind.
Donnelly's bus stops in Anothertown.
Farnham Street clings to the Reformation,
Churches, brick houses and door brass,
Poor Clare Convent, pandemonium in 43 is recalled,
Smells of lunch and early dinner from the hotel,
Maze of Woolworth's counters,
Trays of racing cars, polka-dot footballs,
Cap guns and cork guns, colouring books and paint,
A barmaid sweeps her side of the street,
A man helps a woman across the road
Into Vera Brady's for a new hat and outfit for a wedding.
Corsets laced up the back, litany of cloths …
Shetland wool, camel hair, cashmere,
Cotton, linen, mohair,
Bridge Street for The Lido Café,
Fish and chips, salt and vinegar, a tanner to play the juke-box:

> *The Pub With No Beer*
> *It's lonesome away from your kindred and all*
> *By the campfire at night where the wild dingoes call …*

Night darkens the streets and lanes.
The silence is black.
Sometimes, for no known reasons
We wander in the back gardens of our minds and wonder
Is it love that holds the stars together?
Faraway grains of light sing down on the still night,
Like sparks from long forgotten fires,
Our hearts are warm, our souls reach
For the light and we sense in some small way
How much of life lies hidden faraway.

The boys are playing and playing,
Fiddles, flutes and melodeons,

Hop leap and kick …jig, reel, and jump,
Katie White's out on the street,
Bodhrán beat, thud of her feet,
Waifs in green costumes, lepping and laughing,
Coyle's straw hat all aflame,
With peony roses, lupins and daisies …
Swilling lanes, staggering streets,
Paddy and Pearl stepping it out
Everyone shouting and tripping about

> *Stand back till you see Pearl*
> *With her arse dancing and her face laughing*
> *Go on Pearl …Give it to them*
> *Shake it Pearl*
> *Just look at the length of them legs*
> *And the blood flowing through them*
> *Kripes she's coming down*
> *Give the woman a chair*

> *Any chance of an amhrán eile*
> *From the big curly fella from Clonbrony?*
> > *Duddlie… Diddlie… Dól*
> > *Duddlie… Diddlie… Dól*
> *There's no describing a Fleadh Ceoil.*

Morning drizzle.
Tomato Pat makes a living on less than an acre,
Moving among the lettuce and scallions
In his garden of earthly delight.
Planting, staking, pruning …..
Waiting for the green tomatoes to turn red.
Daydreaming in a strawberry bed,
Ripening into middle age,
School children throw stones at the glasshouse,
The weeds outgrow Tomato Pat, the roots push on …
Ciúnasciúnasciúnasciúnas
The nuns are busy translating silence into Irish.
No matter where you walk, you meet a Ciúnas Sign.

They're everywhere ... on the backs of doors,
Walls, windows, presses, in corridors, porches, toilets ...
And if you think silence matters, so do secrets.
Sister Dolores calls up Tommie Kelly:

> *Don't tell anyone Tommie about the secrets of Fatima.*
> > *That's a good boy ...*
>
> *You know there's only one true God and He's a Catholic*
> *But don't tell the Protestant children anything ...they're not*
> > *entitled to know.*
>
> *I will not Sister. I'll keep my mouth shut.*
> *That's a good boy.*

Authority is in a voice:

> *Seán Ó Bhrádaigh .....Anseo*
> *Tomás Ó Cheallaigh .....Anseo*
> *Nóra Ní Mhainnín.....Anseo.*

Authority is in a black and white habit.
Authority is in the words, *Micheál Seas Suas ...Pól Suigh Síos.*
Authority is in the stick
And there is humiliation round the corner.
If the day at school doesn't add up
Or you are out of luck with spellings
The Dunce's Cap is red with baubles and bells
And you jingle your way through the classes
While the others chant:

> *Duncy, Duncy D*
> *40 Days on A,B,C.*

The Moat belongs to the wind,
Fractal green – daisy wink – twists and curves,
And the Moat belongs to us,
Helps us find our way home in the dark,
Hill of stories,
Once there was ... and once there was not ...
A necklace of seeds,
A head of clay, full of the narrative

Of a wild flower
At the Angelus hour.
St. Patrick with staff in hand,
Looks down on the town.
Everyone looks up at him:
> *On us thy poor children bestow a sweet smile.*

A hawk takes a swipe at a robin
As she feeds her young,
Plucks her feathers, rips her apart,
Life is one great happy meal.
Corpus Christi. Amen.

VII

July.
Fields and fields of buttercups stretch beyond the town.
Wispy hay is blowing in the wind,
White pebbles sleep on dried-up river beds,
Beelzebub, Lord of The Flies orders
All the bugs in the parish to head
For Ward's meadow …clegs …dragonflies …horse-wasps …
Follow the *clipaticlop* … *clipaticlop* of horses
Pulling paddy rakes, wheel rakes,
Men in sunhats, sleeves rolled up,
Are shaking, raking and combing down hay,
The big frightened eyes of a heifer
Look over the ditch at the commotion,
Holy hive and honey,
Blessed are the wild bees swarming above our heads
Will the sun ever come out from the clouds?
A curlew calls from the bottom meadow
Announcing rain,
Fanged flashes, summer thunder,
Ward's men take shelter under the trees
And talk and lean on forks and rakes,
And watch a forage harvester and tandem of silage trucks
Cross the horizon beyond the moat,
Jim Small explains:
> *Hay is a thing of the past, it's silage now,*
> *No work… all machinery .. Doesn't matter if it rains.*
He lights a woodbine, inhales and blows smoke rings
Into a swarm of flies.
News arrives late in the afternoon,
Jane Ward carries a can of tea and sandwiches
And tells the men how –
Mrs. Dorothy Doran who used to take her holidays
In Salthill for the last fifteen summers,
Was found facedown in her breakfast
Of rashers… sausages,…eggs… liver… puddings…
Funeral arrangements later.

For the first two weeks in July
Circus posters are pasted everywhere,
On poles, walls, on a big board at the Market House.
In the early hours the town awakens to almighty engines,
Multi coloured lorries, banjaxed tractors and vans
Pass the Technical School, down the Main Street,
Heading for Keegan's field. The town reaches new heights
As the Big Top rises above the bushes and trees.
Old and young sit around the ring
Staring at the wonders:
Acrobats from Russia, camels from Arabia,
A man eating fire, a girl in tinselled costume
Sparkles like the Queen of Sheba.
> *Are they real people at all?* Janey Early asks.
> *You'd wonder.*
The canon refuses to go and looks the other way.
Pearl Waters runs off with a snake charmer
And returns a month later and tells nobody anything
And everybody wants to know.

VIII

August is fluff in the wind, bearded barley,
Balmy days, the carnival colour of leaves,
Haggards fill up with hay,
Mushrooms appear in Tully's field.
Scent of apples in Walsh's orchard.
Pearl Waters is drying her hair in the sun,
Mary Verdon is plucking at the threads in her cardigan,
Martin Ruther is heading for Camagh Bridge on a bicycle,
Bamboo cane for fishing rod, hooks, worms, line and reel,
Past the ruins of the monastery at Abbeylara
An old man sits by the roadside counting the clouds
And puffing away at his pipe,
Martin inhales the pipe smoke and pushes on.
Boochalawns and thistles everywhere,
Blackberries reach out to the road,
Grasshoppers on their last legs
Vibrate.
Reed music by the riverside,
Water lilies … water-cress … meadowsweet,
Cork bobs, pops, sinks into the dark,
Martin swipes another perch and cycles home,
Swallows gather on the wires,

All the ripening of August.
Briars laden with fruit,
Buckets of blackberries,
And money to be made from the Rag and Boneman
Who buys blackberries by the stone
And sells them to a Dye Factory in the North of Ireland.
A bonus income, a way of paying for school books.
Town's people run down country lanes,
Picking and talking,
Staggering shadows,
Children up on mothers' shoulders reaching for the juicy ones,
Black tongues,

Black blood leaking from cans, pongers, saucepans and buckets.
An old man walks past with a stick
And remembers he was young once
And picked the same berries for the price of a catechism.

Early frost starts to strip the bushes, clothe the roadside.
Pearl Waters wants to be alone,
Something or someone calls her.
She responds, heads up the old road,
Sits on a stone, makes this corner of the world her own,
Breathes the wild breath of country air,
Rocks herself into daydreams of becoming a singer in a band
Her eyes begin to sparkle,
Happy to be close to her dreams if only for an hour
She returns home to face September.

IX

First Thursday in September…The Agricultural Show.
Pink of horse nostrils quivering,
Chestnut, grey, bay and roan,
Duffy's Clydesdale Stallion has
Four white socks to the knees and hocks,
Bulls bellowing …Donkeys braying …Sheep bleating…
Spectators lie on the grass and watch horse and rider
Clear red-white… green-white … blue-white jumps.
The loudspeaker calls out:
>   *Number 5 has four faults*
>   *Number 7 is eliminated.*
>   *Will stewards please keep spectators outside the arena.*
>   *Will the owner of the Aberdeen Angus bull number 55*
>   *Please go to the Tea Marquee immediately*
>   *As the animal is causing an obstruction.*

Housewives examine the poultry coops,
Hear the hens cackle, ducks quack,
Tables of exhibits in the Big Marquee,
Lilies-of-the-valley and machinery,
Prizes for oats, wheat and barley,
Janey Early whispers to Mrs. Farrelly:
>   *Did you hear?*
> *What?*
>   *About Mrs. Blaney,*
> *What?*
>   *She won 1st prize for her gooseberry jam.*
> *That mad bitch.*

Further prizes for flower arrangements …dressmaking and crochet …
Outside the marquee a Trick of The Loop is
Waving a Bullroarer and shouting:
>   *Ollie …Ollie Ollie Ollie Ollie*
>   *My Granny's Granny is shouting down from heaven at me*
>   *And I'm shouting up at her*
>   *We're all bobbing here …We're all bobbing here*

The last few tickets here ...pick a straw
Even numbers you win
Uneven you lose
I'm not making a fortune missus ...I'm only making a living
God made the bees
The bees make the honey
The jockey does the dirty work
And the Bookie takes the money .....
Hawkers put down their baskets
To gawk at The Stone Wall Championship.
Gormley's mare clears 6 foot 6 inches to take the cup.

Monday is market day,
Old ridges and furrows yield in Autumn,
A countryside of tillers and sowers invade the town.
Lines of carts, orange and blue shafts raised,
Tied horses with winkers on
Regain their composure outside the Market House.
Blotchy faces, stubbled faces, haggle over money,
Words devouring words, noise everywhere
The click of studs on stone
Young lads shovel spuds, sleeves rolled up,
Globules of sweat on their foreheads.
The whole place is reeking of plug tobacco,
Men wearing caps spit out phlegm,
Old decency in felt hats knows better
Some are in fits of laughter, others recall the year of bad oats:
    All straw and no grain.
Sacks of
Wheat, oats and barley against the wall
Await collection,
The giant iron weighing scales crashes down
With a clank.
Old Dooley is chewing a wisp of straw and talking of drawkie days,
Martin Ruther is eating a thick slice of bread and looking on,
Roddy Gilpen starts up the tractor
And Market Street disappears in the smoke.

X

It is truly Autumn.
Trees are shedding old life, leaf by leaf,
Over the hills and far away.
Fields are struggling to be green,
Under a stark grey sky,
The wind is ripping posters off the Market House.
Orion the hunter has returned,
Migrating geese fly in from Canada,
A hare hides in the after-grass,
The Carneys are snagging turnips below us.
Lily from the Hill of Molly slips in a furrow,
With a bag of potatoes on her back.
Cock Fagan never took the boat to Hollyhead last Spring.

> *Me back is broken from picking spuds in Tully's field.*
> *I'm definitely out of here …*
> *This time for sure …*
> *Any day now …*
> *As soon as …*
> *If only …*
> *What if …*
> *On top of Old Smoky, all covered with snow*
> *I lost my true lover, for courtin' too slow.*

He returns to the drills and continues picking potatoes.
Sister Flahoolagh distributes free boots and jumpers
To the needy children in the school.
Peter Daly, cattle drover, walks three heifers home
From the fair in Arva in the dark.
Mary Major weighs tea and sugar
And puts the tea into red bags and sugar in brown bags,
Before she closes the shop.
Susan Fox looks into a teacup
Janey Early desires to know the future:

> *What do you see Susan?*
> *I see the stars, black stars on a white dome.*
> *I see the tail that wags the dog.*
> *I see a bunch of keys. Are you thinking of leaving?*

> *There's a tree looking into your bedroom… the branches*
> *Are stretching in to help you.*
> *You're going on a journey but it's … not far.*
> *You'll pass water…before you cross it.*
> *There's a silver fish down here. That's money for you.*
> *How much money? How much…?*
> *Ah! It won't be hard to spend it.*

Susan strikes the dome of the cup on the palm of her hand
Roads of tealeaves freewheel down the side
The words fall out:

> *Is that a heel? No*
> *It's a hare fleeing across a field*
>   *I don't like hares.*
> *Well it could be a rabbit. It's hard to tell.*

One day in Autumn.
While the crows were circling the beech trees,
And wind and rain would go through you,
Old Jamsie McDonagh recalls his past.
Distant fire by the roadside, tent full of children,
Piebald mare tied to a bush, old bitch of a dog,
Pulling herself away from her pups.
He remembers his father walloping tin cans, his mother
Staring into the smoke,
And Julie, his older sister,
Wearing a pony tail and walking the byroads
In search of:

> *A lock of hay for the pony … any praties or bread?*
> *God Bless You.*

Guards' wives, farmer's wives, the butcher's wife
Assemble in Moxham Street Hall
For the A.G.M. of the I.C.A.
Women wanting to be alone
Happy to be away from their men
If only for awhile.
Sharing recipes for Chicken Marengo

Joint and skin chicken and put into casserole
Heat oil, add onion and cook for a few minutes
Add tomato purée and cornflour and mix well
Rub through a sieve ...
        Rub what?
Shouts Mrs. Muldoon
And the whole class of women erupts into
A sea of laughter, tears falling from their eyes
Their boobs shaking in their bras,
Laughing themselves silly
Taking the rage out of their lives
They return to their homes renewed
Ready to start another day.

Mickey Maguire lives on his own
With the moon and stars for neighbours,
Grows garlic on the window sill
To keep his madness out,
Walks to town with his head down
To buy a loaf of bread.
Once he ate clay, drank rusty water
And had to be taken away in an ambulance.
Mickey makes darkness his secret,
Imagines he has committed some unpardonable sin,
Walks the dark roads and laneways,
Talks to the hoarse wind in the trees
And asks for forgiveness.

Kindling fires on the Scrabby Road,
Magpie morning music on the terrace roofs,
Women and small children gather round
Pat McGiver's van,
Back doors swing open to the creamery can,
Chattering wives ... clattering cans
Pushing and shouting for pints ... quarts
Milk for babies' bottles ...

An extra sup for the cat, Pat.
Ladle dip sings into the can
Scoop and souse … one woman shouts:
Go on Pat don't be mane,
Some talk, more overhear conversations:
A man made money once
And when he was dying, he ate it with his toast for breakfast,
Then up and died and took the money with him.
The ten o'clock news blares from the radio in the van.
Someone shouts:
Will you look at Ward's dog with his thing up Finnan's Darky
Dirty dogs …Dirty dogs …

The mornings are foggy,
Leaves grow darker and darker,
Apples are ready to fall
The river is swallowing her banks
Farmers come in from the fields
One car passes another quietly at the top of the hill
Clouds block out the blue of the sky,
Two boys raise their chestnuts in combat in the school yard
Rattle of chestnuts … tangle of shoe laces
Splutter splatter of Martin's champion,
Loud laughter from the other boys gathered round.
Flicker of light from the fiery skull of a turnip,
The clocks go back; street lamps come on.
All of a sudden it's cold.
Mary Green and Dirty Jimmy are bedding down together
In Heslin's stable.
October fights against the dark.

XI

A wet November night creeps in.
The town gossips about the dead,
Cockroaches run across Rosset Kelly's floor,
And he informs us:
> *You know, death isn't voluntary,*
As he stamps on the cockroaches with his size tens.
An older house talks to a bungalow
Over the frozen hills:
> *Where did you get such a name?*
The bungalow doesn't reply.
Philomena can't sleep at night,
Her secret intentions weren't answered.
Owl-eyed night.
Restless spirits walk the roads,
Dead leaves ride the wind
Stray across the road.
Winter rain floods the fields,
Hoop and cloot marks of the cattle in wet gaps,
The haggard is all muck and clábhar.
> *Does anyone know the business of sin?*
Indulgences are a one day industry in this town,
Plenary and Partial available for souls in need
To cut the cost of suffering of our dear departed
Good bargains to be had : 300 days ... 500 days less
If we intercede on their behalf and pay and pray a little.
Clochcinn, dormitory for the dead,
Whispering and counting prayers and calculating
Souls' release from Purgatory.
Rosset Kelly wants to know:
> *How come the Protestants never have to pay*
> *For their Departed?*
Old Dooley isn't sure of the whole business:
> *Those who know never tell us,*
> *Those who tell us never know.*
Fr. Woods quietly talks to the congregation:

As we enter the darkness of winter we need to put to rest
Our fears and worries about the next life,
Our concern for our dear departed relatives and friends.
We remember the ghosts of the departed
Who have no relations to pray for them.
Not only should we put the dead to rest in November
We need to meet with our own ghosts
That which is truly wild and hurting us,
Let us confront the rage within us,
Bring it for a winter walk to the country roads,
We can listen to the wind in the trees
After awhile you'll find the trees have less to say
And settle into being trees
And you'll settle into being yourself again,
It's good to walk the country roads
When you don't know what else to do.

Canon O'Kane looks sharply at Fr. Woods,
Canon O'Kane has the final words:

Requiem aeternum dona eis Domine
Et lux perpetua luceat eis.

XII

A December evening
Is growing frost on the trees and bushes,
All the house lights climb the hill,
Little windows barely open,
Like mouths in sleep.
Christmas advertisements on the TV sing:
>   *Tom Thumb cigars for Christmas … Tom Thumbs in tins of ten …*
Blue and red edged envelopes arrive from America with dollars.
The first Christmas Cards are on the mantelpiece,
Holly and ivy wedged behind the pictures.
Mother and son go shopping for Christmas,
All the way down to Morrissey's for
Sultanas…raisins …lemon peel …nutmeg …cherries …almonds
In Pettit's they fill another bag with:
2lb. pots of red jam and a bottle of brown sauce,
Lemon jelly …sponge cake …custard, sherry and cream for the trifle
Mother and son return home, shopping bags full
Past a pool of streetlight at the crossroads
They face the dark road home with a flashlight.

Mrs. Farrelly has made her Christmas puddings
Her son Terry has had his gallbladder out for Christmas
And will have to be watching what he's eating.
Busty Mahety is killing turkeys with a brush handle
And plucking day and night
And Mary Verdon is dreaming of dying before Christmas
But that happens every year.

Busty Mahety joins Hughie Small and The Danger Smith
In The Star Bar.
The three men get triumphantly drunk for Christmas.
Danger Smith strikes up a conversation with his empty glass
The glass doesn't reply
And at that critical moment

The glass jumps off the counter
And shatters itself on the floor
So Danger Smith insists.
Busty Mahety is having remorse
For all the turkeys he's killing
And starts getting all sentimental
He tells the others:
> One turkey looked me straight in the eye
> When her turn came for the broom handle.
> I couldn't do it. I have her in the bag here
> Look at her, pure nature's intelligence
> Birds and animals know more than we do
> They can sense a storm on the way … know all about the weather.

Hughie Small states:
> The tractor in a wonderful loco… motive.
Then he complains:
> There's never enough light at Christmas
> To find your way home in the dark.
Outside, the three men cling to one another.
The streets sway; houses swing from the trees.
Mahety's turkey jumps out of the bag
And takes wings up Water Lane
Hughie Small squares up to Rosset's cat on Moxham Street:
> Psh … Psh … Psh …Psh …
> Good Night, Mrs. Cat
> Are we going to have a white Christmas?
The town sleeps,
All the doors and windows close in secrets.
Tonight above all nights everyone feels a sense of belonging.
Purple chasuble, white chasuble …
Are all in accord with Bethlehem.
The town awakens
To little remote stars on her ceiling
The streets throw shadows, the grass on the Moat is black.
> Much talked about snow never comes.
So old Dooley says.

Martin Ruther
Gets a small box of water-colour paints
And a mouth organ in his stocking.
The whole town is heading for Bethlehem on the hill.
Some walking, more driving the roads
Carrying their dark secrets
To place them in the crib.
The school children's voices are raised in song:
     Oíche chiúin, oíche Mhic Dé,
Janey Early prays out loud:
     Hail Holy queen mother of mercy,
     Hail our life our sweetness and our hope …
Other prayers are soft whisperings, babble of Babel,
For all are seated here: compassion … endurance …blind faith ….
A shopkeeper fingers his pocket
Pretends he's counting his coppers
When someone gives him the wicked eye.
Pearl Waters clings to the rails
But everyone recalls her wild dance,
The town and its mother know Pearl.
All stare at the crib as if it was a cage
With ox and ass and baby in the straw
But few can see the bars.

Too much of Christmas.
Too much of the Galilean
More of us pray to a different god.
With a paper hat and a cracker
We're full of goose, turkey, ham and stuffing,
Too much to drink
And much of the same on the box:
The Queen's speech, the Pope's blessing and Billy Smart's circus,
Time to be moving on.

Night is going on outside,
All the houses close their eyes
Against the darkness.

The town as theatre of laughter and heartbreak
Turns in its sleep and sings:
    The wren, the wren, the King of all birds.
        The wren is the only bird
        That sings all year round.
    We'll hunt the wren cries Robin the Bobbin.
        The wren is the only bird
        That sings all year round.
    Stone the wren to death.
        That sings all year round.
    Carry the bird's brain through the streets
    Up Waterlane, down Silver Street.
        The wren is the only bird
        That sings all year round.

The town lies still
Children are sardined into a bed,
Three at the top, two at the bottom.
Rosset Kelly is waiting for the cat to purr,
Mary Verdon closes her eyelids,
Faraway voices return to her
To protect her from what life throws at her daily.
She hears ghosts talking in her sleep,
She sees them
Polishing the snow, parcelling up the wind.
Night sleeps with daylight on either side,
The wind blows leaves through our dreams,
Leaves, like lost words
From long forgotten conversations.
The trees stand their ground,
The branches barely whisper.
Milk white flakes flood the morning,
Busty Mahety tries to put his trousers on
Upside down
He tries again and gets it right.
Doors squeak open
Another year begins.

About the author

NOEL MONAHAN has won numerous awards for his poetry and writing. His awards include: The SeaCat National Poetry Award, organised by Poetry Ireland, the RTE P.J. O'Connor Award, the ASTI Achievements Award, The Hiberno-English Poetry Award and The Irish Writers' Union Poetry Award. His poetry is prescribed text for LEAVING CERTIFICATE ENGLISH, due for examination in  2011 and 2012. *Curve of The Moon* is Noel Monahan's fifth collection of poetry. *Opposite Walls* was published in 1991, *Snowfire* in 1995, *Curse of The Birds* in 2000 and *The Funeral Game* in 2004, all published by Salmon. His most recent play, *The Children of Lir*, was performed by Livin Dred Theatre and directed by Padraig McIntyre. Noel Monahan holds an M.A. in Creative Writing.